ALTERED LANDSCAPES
The Photographs of John Pfahl

ALTERED LANDSCAPES
The Photographs of John Pfahl

Introduction by
Peter C. Bunnell

Published by The Friends of Photography
in association with Robert Freidus Gallery

ISSN 0163-7916; ISBN 0-933286-23-6
Library of Congress Catalogue Card No. 81-66455.

ACKNOWLEDGEMENTS

In approaching the landscape, the problem faced by photographers has been seen as one of discovering and defining, within the four edges of the frame, equivalences between the land as raw material, the artist as a creative being and the potentials of the medium itself. When the artist is unsuccessful the viewer forms a direct relationship with the subject rather than with the photograph. At those other times when an equivalence is reached, however, the photograph becomes an image that transcends specific subject matter. While their subjects exist, these images are not literal.

One of the enduring traditions within landscape photography has rested on this emotional alteration of the subject to make an image, but at the same time it has denied the option of any physical alteration of the landscape. John Pfahl has challenged that assumption by physically changing the pictured environment and by creating an extended series of altered landscapes. This series combines wit and elegance in ways that reaffirm our belief that art needs artists, not rules. To be sure, there have been those throughout the medium's history who have fabricated photographs. Intentionally creating subjects that previously existed only in the artists' mind they have moved closer to the strategies of other art media. While the fabrication of photographs has even become commonplace in recent years, no other body of work approaches Pfahl's in its conceptual and visual richness.

Pfahl made the photographs contained in *Untitled 26* during the second half of the 1970s. The series, *Altered Landscapes,* has proved to be very popular with curators, critics and collectors. We are pleased to bring a substantial number of them together in this volume. During the photographer's visit to Carmel in December 1980, John and I selected and sequenced the prints. Production began on this book, which is being published in conjunction with an exhibition of Pfahl's photographs at The Friends of Photography's gallery in Carmel from April 10 to May 10, 1981.

I would especially like to thank John Pfahl for his wonderful cooperation and enthusiasm throughout the entire project. Warm thanks also to Peter Bunnell, whose insightful introduction not only contributes to our understanding of the pictures, but firmly places Pfahl's work in the context of contemporary photography. Thanks to Robert Freidus for his generous support and to his associates at the Freidus Gallery, Janet Borden and Richard Pollinger. Also assisting with preparations for the exhibition and/or book were Stuart Rome, Nancy Gonchar, Theresa Miller and Charles Stainback. Thanks to The Friends' staff: to David Featherstone for another fine job in copy editing and in organizing the exhibition, to Peter Andersen for his exacting and beautiful design of the book, and to Debbie Bradburn, Libby McCoy, Nancy Ponedel and Mary Virginia Swanson. Finally, thanks to our fine printers, Dave Gardner and his staff at Gardner/Fulmer Lithograph, for their handsome four-color laser-scanner reproductions. We are pleased to share John Pfahl's *Altered Landscapes.*

James Alinder, Editor
The Untitled *Series*

Triangle, Bermuda, 1975

INTRODUCTION

Peter C. Bunnell

A keystone in the arch of human understanding is the recognition that man at certain critical points synthesizes experience. Another way of stating this is that man learns while he sees and what he learns influences what he sees.

Edward T. Hall
The Hidden Dimension

One of the concepts regarding photography and the making of photographs that has taken the longest to be realized and appreciated is that of intentional creation. Early in this century the pictorialists began to articulate the inherent linkage between the act of photographing, the sense of responsibility that falls on photographers because of their pictures and the sensuality of the pictures themselves. These are the principles that have become the fundamental bases of modern photography. Further, photographs that were once derided as illustrative are today not so disrespected because this term is no longer reserved to describe work reinforcing traditional regimes. It now refers to that providing an illustration or a kind of mechanical for the activity Edward Hall identifies above. The art of successful photography has once again come to be concerned with artifice and, like the best writers of literature, the goal of a contemporary photographer like John Pfahl is not to turn viewers into rereaders but into readers.

John Pfahl was born in New York in 1939 and grew up in rural New Jersey. He began his interest in photography at Syracuse University, where he was a student enrolled in a program of advertising and graphic design. Importantly, his earliest work was in color. Following two years in the Army he worked for commercial photographers in New York City and in California. In 1966 he returned to Syracuse and studied color photography, graduating two years later with a Master's Degree. He has been on the faculty of the Rochester Institute of Technology since 1968. From 1969 through 1974 he made three-dimensional screen-printed photographs on formed plastic. From 1974 through 1978 he worked on an extensive series of related unmanipulated color photographs on the theme of *The Altered Landscape.* These photographs form the substance of this book.

Music I, Ellicottville, New York, 1974

While working with the musician and composer David Gibson, Pfahl became interested in photographing elements placed in the actual landscape. Deciding to make collaborative photographic music scores, they went out into the forest south of Buffalo, New York, where Pfahl resides, applied tape to trees and executed two compositions together. The intention, though never realized, was that the visual configuration was to be recorded in notation form and played. The photographic image would serve as a visual backdrop to the musicians. While Pfahl now considers these two pieces to be largely unresolved, they mark the starting point for his later conceptions. *Music I,* reproduced here, is one of these two initial efforts.

Pfahl rapidly became interested in the pictorial potential of these alterable acts and has now formed a body of some one hundred and fifty images in this series. The idea was not acted upon immediately, however. It was not until the summer of 1975, at the Penland School in North Carolina, that he executed ten works, including *Shed with Blue Dotted Lines,* illustrated here in color as the finished work and in black and white as a straight reference photograph to show the actual construct of the blue tape assemblage on the doors.

The photographer describes the notions of the pictures in his series as follows: "The added elements suggest numerous mark-making devices associated with photographs, maps, plans and diagrams. On different occasions, they may pointedly repeat a strong formal element in the landscape (i.e. the outline of large rocks echoed in rope in *Outlined Boulders,* page 37); they may fill in information suggested by the scene (the red line in *Coconut Palm,*

left: *Shed with Blue Dotted Lines, Penland, North Carolina, 1975;* right: *Site Documentation*

page 51, or the yellow ropes in the meadow in *Haystack Cone,* page 41); they may depend upon information external to the photograph itself (the location of Bermuda in *Triangle,* page 8 and in a black-and-white reference print, page 13); or, finally, they may be only arbitrarily related to the scene (as in *Pink Rock Rectangle,* page 17, where the granite boulders simply form the substrate for an imposed figure)."[1]

In these pictures Pfahl creates, usually within twenty or thirty feet of his camera, a construction that is given order and perfection through the manipulation of the optics of the camera. These fabrications may be made with tape, string, rope or foil positioned on or amongst the objects in the picture or through the placement of objects, such as balls, in the foreground plane. Pfahl manipulates these illusions carefully and tediously, often making preparatory drawings on a black-and-white Polaroid of the scene or using clear plastic overlays on the ground glass itself. In all of this there is the critical notion that the arrangements are not done to mathematical perfection but are purely visual. He has pointed out that his working method demonstrates the fact that since we cannot see the flat picture plane through the ground glass of a view camera we must work with pictures, in this case the Polaroid, to adjust both the mind and the construction to the picture making problem. Utmost care is taken not to alter the actual subject in a way Pfahl would consider harmful to his positivist respect for nature. He has described his process as the "possession of the space and then its return to a pure state following my own personal ritual"; he approaches the entire endeavor with a "strategy of affection".[2]

Much has been written about the *Altered Landscape* series. Pfahl himself has commented most informatively in a number of interviews on his background, techniques and intentions.[3] The term *picturesque* frequently appears in these interviews. As a concept the picturesque is very much aligned to the illustrative. Were it not for the unfortunately bad name the given to it during the late nineteenth century, we would realize that the picturesque was originally understood in the context of the striking picture. This interpretation has been overlooked and therefore much of the reason why John Pfahl's photographs are important has been missed. I believe Pfahl's photographs are important; they are very picturesque because they suggest to me his immense pleasure in making them and his ready, indeed, his eager acceptance of responsibility for them.

These pictures are a celebration of both the photographer's art and his deliberateness. Their quality lies in the demonstration of forcing nature to rival art. By addressing his camera to scenes that he feels, as some others do, are on the edge of cliché or novelty, he actually imposes more of himself than might otherwise be the case. Now Pfahl is not a passing entertainer, but a fervent artist who has worked hard at the detail and the mastery of his craft. He has lifted it from the drudgery that characterizes so much of what is termed concept art. In a recent lecture Isaac Beshavis Singer remarked, "In art, like in love, the act and the enjoyment must go together. If there is a redemption in literature, it must be imminent. In contrast to politics, art does not thrive on promises. If it does not impress you now, it never will."[4] Such is the case with the art of John Pfahl.

To be put off by these pictures is somewhat akin to rejecting the idea that we can never subtract from knowledge but only add to it. Pfahl's contribution comes to us through the true pleasure of his wit and his doctrine of spotless technique. In the sense that these pictures reflect the individual ego of their creator they are expressionistic. While the obviousness of the demonstrated acts—stringing rope, laying tape, wrapping foil—might be seen as only superficial, these gestures, like the gestures of contrivance in any medium, reveal the inner artist. As was suggested earlier, this revelation is particularly difficult for a photographer, considering the traditional inhibitions against methods which have, for too long, only served the basic banality of photographic representation.

Pfahl's imagery is a sure manifestation of the belief that society can produce an art suitable to its nature and, in this case, a specific kind of photographic presence that expresses current societal values. What can be seen in Pfahl's work is a certain and not so subtle anti-popularization that seeks to subdue the rude realities of the 1960s with a beauty more ideal and a morality rather more precious than what was then current. It is removed from contemporaneity and, by reinstituting values and conventions of the past within a mode of thinking about the present, Pfahl creates a revivalist photography. The photographs are scientific in nature

Site Documentation: Triangle, Bermuda, 1975

in that they build their esteem on a mathematical system of perspective and illusion through a precise and unmoving point of view. This anti-emotionalism seeks to re-establish a more rigid self consciousness of photographic perspective than has been the case with the rash of modernist distortions found, for instance, in aerial photographs, street photographs and decontextualized details in the 1950s.

Pfahl's reasoning is rooted in an interest in the problems of spatial positioning current among contemporary anthropologists. Instead of finding fault with distortions, orthogonals that converge too quickly or grossly enlarged objects in the picture plane, these optical characteristics have become the topography of Pfahl's argument. What is new is the immensely sharp awareness of the effects the positioning of the camera might produce in non-pictorial terms, that is, for concerns outside the substrata of interest in the scene itself. This is why his photographs are so very different from the modernist notions revealed, for instance by Alvin Langdon Coburn in his well-known photograph *Octopus* (1912) or in his writing:

> . . . why should not the camera also throw off the shackles of conventional representation? . . . Why not repeated successive exposures of an object in motion on the same plate? Why should not perspective be studied from angles hitherto

13

neglected or unobserved? . . . Think of the joy of doing something which it would be impossible to classify, or to tell which was the top and which was the bottom![5]

It would seem that in Pfahl's photographs the entire question of the construction of pictorial space has been replaced, as if to prepare us for the last quarter of our century during which we must, as perhaps in no time in years, consider what is retinal and what is perceived. Our momentary, fragmented and captured vision of disorder and emotion has been replaced by a cool rendering of purposefulness as if to accord another dimension of positivism to the moving force of contemporary human awareness. Pfahl's work is an attack on the problems of space and, ultimately, existence from a rational point of view. Whether Pfahl has read Leonardo's *Trattato* I do not know, but it would not surprise me if he has. Pfahl's work is hidden from us only in the sense that what he does before the exposure is never revealed. We do not go through his work step by step, incident by incident, to discern the way it was constructed as if one were taking a timepiece apart, because what Pfahl is doing is putting the watch together. If we need to investigate these pictures it is only to address the issue of three-dimensional realities subjected to two-dimensional photographic surfaces.

Pfahl's work rests at a point in the latter part of the continuum of art's development in which has been reflected man's growing awareness first of himself, second of his environment, then of himself scaled to his environment and, finally, of the transaction between himself and his environment. Pfahl's photographs are but one more demonstration of man's inhabitation of many different perceptual worlds; they tell more about man than they provide simple data on human perception. They are not shocking in the sense that some photographs, and most modern paintings have been shocking, because they do not conform to the popular notion of perception in art. Rather, they ply the delicate balance between understanding and expectation. This point of traverse is the most contemporary aspect about Pfahl's work, which I hesitate to describe with the now fashionable term *post-modern;* it symbolizes the vastly changed world of today where ridding the viewer of radical expectation has allowed the artist to reveal himself through intellectual process.

His photographs are static in that they do not reflect the traditional view of looking out of a large plate-glass window (a frequent analogy for photographs and a pictorial device now used by him in his most recent photographs) because of the simple fact that the images allow no movement. Not only is it improper to move one's body or head to see more, there is simply no more to see. It is just the reverse demand which Pfahl places upon us: to remain still, focused and unmoving. The glorious color, sometimes pushed to the extreme of decorativeness and verisimilitude, only enhances the tension created by this forced inhibition of movement, a restraint that fully recognizes our need to see a picture and not recreate an experience. The picture is the experience.

Will we ever reach the point where we might believe that we dissect nature along lines laid down by our photographers? Although few accept this proposition, and Susan Sontag cautions us when she writes, "photography implies that we know about the world if we accept it as the camera records it",[6] I do not find it a poor proposition at all. Much as we have come to understand nature through our native languages—a fact long held—I do not believe that photographs, let alone paintings, are unacceptable forms of instruction that might serve this understanding. In such a context one could move meaningfully to the apprehension not only of nature, but of subtle differences in cultural view by studying the photographs of Emerson, Atget, Moholy, Stieglitz, Adams and Pfahl, to suggest a list pertinent to this thought. Photographs such as these reflect a patience and a chore in teaching such that they are demanding, and give back to Pfahl the role of one who elucidates discovery through creativity.

John Pfahl has become an influential photographer. In a most straightforward way the fastidiousness of his color imagery together with its lush descriptiveness has fostered the development of the genre. Quite apart from this obvious impact, however, has been his influence as an educated and articulate artist. He has rejected the cult of naiveté, of working without preconceptions. His own purposefulness has given us a break in the rigidity of convention; his sense of history and his sense of learning have put photography back on track. He is a stylist. He has not been afraid to reveal what he knows, or to reveal his learning states; for him each picture had to have its own reason. "It had to be more than simply a new illusion—the illusion has never been the main point."[7] In this way John Pfahl is not a magician or an illusionist. He is an artist who favors the elegance of the mind that appreciates reality.

NOTES

1. John Pfahl, "Introduction," Focal Point Productions Slide Set, Rochester, New York, 1977.

2. Interview with the author, Princeton, New Jersey, November 24, 1980.

3. Anthony Bannon, "John Pfahl's Picturesque Paradoxes," *Afterimage,* February, 1979, pp. 10-13 (including transcript of interview).

   Van Deren Coke, *Fabricated to be Photographed* (San Francisco: San Francisco Museum of Modern Art, 1979), pp. 9-10.

   Ben Lifson, "You Can Fool Some of the Eyes Some of the Time," *The Village Voice,* March 6, 1978, p. 68.

   Stuart Rome, "Interview with John Pfahl, Sun Valley, Idaho, June, 1980," *Northlight,* Number 14, 1981.

4. "I.B. Singer, at West Point, Meets Cadets of Another World," *New York Times,* September 25, 1980, p. B12.

5. Alvin Langdon Coburn, "The Future of Pictorial Photography" (1916), *A Photographic Vision* (Salt Lake City: Peregrine Smith, 1980), pp. 194-195.

6. Susan Sontag, *On Photography* (New York: Farrar, Straus and Giroux, 1977), p. 23.

7. *Op.cit.,* Interview.

PETER C. BUNNELL is David Hunter McAlpin Professor of the History of Photography and Modern Art at Princeton University. He is the author of numerous books and articles on photography, including a recently published volume on pictorialism, A Photographic Vision *(Peregrine Smith, 1980).*

Pink Rock Rectangle, Lewiston, New York, 1975

Red Right Angle, Buffalo, New York, 1975

Blue Right Angle, Buffalo, New York, 1978

Library Projection, Tampa, Florida, 1977

Necker Cube, Penland, North Carolina, 1975

Slanting Orange Lines, Route 17, New York, 1975

Blue X, Pembroke, New York, 1975

top left: Roan Mountain Lightning, Roan Mountain, North Carolina, 1977; *top right:* Mangrove Swamp Lightning, Matheson Hammock, Florida, 1977; *bottom left:* Bamboo Lightning, Penland, North Carolina, 1977; *bottom right:* Snow Creek Lightning, Wing, North Carolina, 1977

top left: Aspen Lightning, Frisco, Colorado, 1977; *top right:* White Lightning, Delle, Utah, 1977;
bottom left: Volcano Lightning, Kilauea Volcano, Hawaii, 1978;
bottom right: Live Oak Lightning, Lompoc, California 1978

Foil Rocks, Lewiston, New York, 1975

Slanting Forest, Lewiston, New York, 1975

Australian Pines, Fort DeSoto, Florida, 1977

Leigh Lake Circle, Grand Teton National Park, Wyoming, 1977

Six Oranges, Buffalo, New York, 1975

Bagel Pile, South Buffalo, New York, 1976

Nine Desert Snowballs, Hell's Half Acre, Wyoming, 1977

33

Tracks, Bonneville Salt Flats, Utah, 1977

Vertical Highway, Lone Pine, California, 1976

Mountain Triangle, Death Valley Junction, California, 1976

Outlined Boulders, Red Rock Canyon, California, 1976

Blue Grid, Pembroke, New York, 1977

Red Setters in Red Field, Charlotte, North Carolina, 1976

Moose and Arrow, Grand Teton National Park, Wyoming, 1977

Haystack Cone, Freeport, Maine, 1976

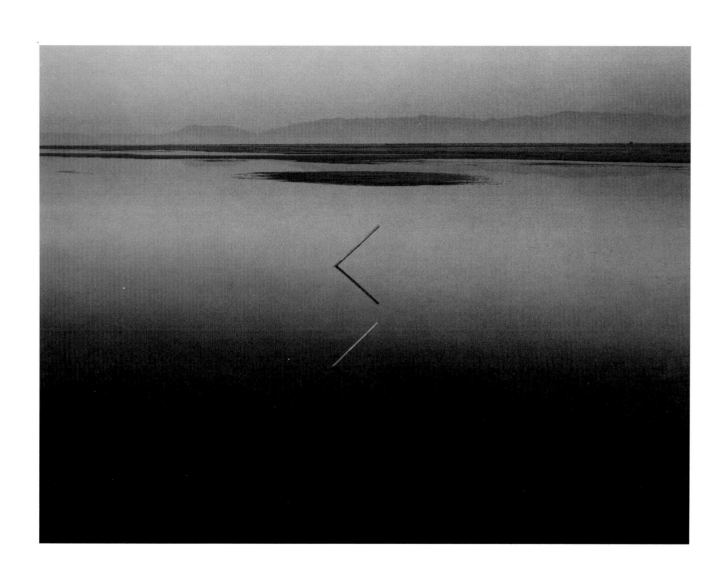

Great Salt Lake Angles, Great Salt Lake, Utah, 1977

Monument Valley with Red String, Monument Valley, Utah, 1977

Red Rock Repeat, Torrey, Utah, 1977

Big Dipper, Charlotte, North Carolina, 1976

Moonrise over Pie Pan, Capitol Reef National Park, Utah, 1977

Black Rock Hill with Diagonal Lines, Death Valley, California, 1976

Canyon Point, Zion Canyon National Park, Utah, 1977

Tree and Mountain Cleft, Boulder, Colorado, 1977

Coconut Palm Horizon, Kona Coast, Hawaii, 1978

Wave, Lave, Lace, Pescadero Beach, California, 1978

Wave Theory I-IV, Puna Coast, Hawaii, 1978

Wave Theory V, Puna Coast, Hawaii, 1977

THE FRIENDS OF PHOTOGRAPHY

The Friends of Photography, founded in 1967, is a not-for-profit membership organization with headquarters in Carmel, California. The Friends actively supports and encourages creative photography through wide-ranging programs in publications, grants and awards to photographers, exhibitions, workshops, lectures and critical inquiry. The publications of The Friends, the primary benefit received by members of the organization, emphasize contemporary photography yet are also concerned with the criticism and history of the medium. They include a monthly newsletter, a quarterly journal and major photographic monographs. Membership is open to everyone. To receive an informational membership brochure write to the Membership Director, The Friends of Photography, Post Office Box 500, Carmel, California 93921.